"Nothing is so soothing to the mind than inheriting a cursed gift that turns into a blessing."

This edition published by Creapac publishers.
Dirschauerstr 14
10245 Berlin

ISBN : 978 3 947650 90 3
CREAPAC

Poetry Simplified
Quotes and Short Stories
By
S. Svikiro

Also by Andy I. Svikiro

I CAME IN BLIND

SHADES OF AFFILIATION

PRINCESS ANENI

GRANDPA'S VILLAGE
STORIES

200 LOGICAL ANSWERS
FOR EVERY WOMAN

TAKA' DREAMS
BOOK 1
BOOK 2
BOOK 3
BOOK 4

Contents:

Loveable Woman 1

Spiritual Call 2

Village Foot 3-4

Quotes 5-6

Labour of love 7-9

Abandoned 10

Ms Perfectionist 11-12

Tough Love 13-14

Dip them 15-16

Dilemma 17-18

Double Reflection 19

Gone by.15 20

A glass short 21

A good man 22

Immigrant 23-24

Quotes 25-26

I still dream 27-28

Artificial Death 29-30

I came in blind 31-34

Quotes 35-36

Tell it to her 37-38

Cravity 39

Tears of a child 40-42

Shades of affiliation 43-46

Python tales 47-48

Adopted life 49

Quotes 50

Trader's worship 51-52

Before I depart 53

The door 54

Morning prayer 55

Last Hope 56-62

Quote 63-64

Misfortune 65

Stillborn 66

Take a plunge 67

Sparrow 68

A farmer's dilemma 69-70

Childhood friends 71-72

Quotes 73-74

Against the wall 75-81

A mother's love can be a curse 82

A female bear 83-84

On your own 85

Words from Aunty 86

Blood is thicker 87-81

Blindsided 89

Family 90

A bug 91

Man up 92

Thoughts 93-94

Berlin 95-97

Quotes 98

Something strange out there 99

Quotes 100

Loveable Woman

Plain and simple
Sleeps like no other
Her beauty reveals her heart
Skin as smooth as her words
Her courage and confidence walk next to her,
The sun, that shines upon her, leaves no shadow
Was she born, out of a woman or she slid out of a
shell
The way she views the world, is in her step
She neither despises nor condemns,
blames it all, on the nature of life

Disturbed by lost souls, selfish
in their gains
She wishes nothing but happiness
The butterflies adore her
The green grass smiles as it
feels her warmth and kindness
She knows no love, for she is love herself
Her heart cannot be broken, it pounds
and fits in every shape and form

The wind clears her path
leaving a trail of golden platted roses
The dust swallows itself
as the bugs retreat into their holes
She is a pure beauty, a rare stone
Dazzles you if you dare stare
Miles underneath the sea, her soul
searches for purity yet the sea seeks
her presence for all eyes to see

Spiritual Call

ulululululululuuuuoooo
The mouth ululates as the feet stomp
The knees buckle as the toes dig
holding the heels and swaying the hips
The eyes glow twisting the body and
pumping the heart
The pores clot wrecking the nerves and
spinning the head
Rhythm is lost, as
the cheeks fall and sight is gone
You tremble and moan
Whimpering in praise
They are here, the rulers of the
Kingdom
The fathers of the earth
The whole village erupts
ulululululululuuuuoooo
A spiritual call that nourishes the ground
That strengthens the bond
A call that appeases the spirits

Village Girl

Cracks of lakes flow beneath her bare feet
A mackerel calls it home, gasping for air
Through her toe, a blue Lagoon emerges
As the storm sweeps by, dust settles
suffocating the breeds, forcing the spiders
to flee their egged webs
Every thud destabilizes the entire network
The lake dries, creating narrow thin streams
filled with a mysteious fog

The dark bark reaches a point of no return
cutting its way into thick grass
Wasps whispers and flee in dozens
Its strength can sharpen a blunt knife
as it is a weapon
Snails find joy harboring underneath
its great shade
Like all living creatures, the first born
is the biggest and the boldest
The young ones line up according to
their sizes and strength, none is sparred the
wrath of a hardened ground, shared with existing
friendly mammals

A misstep, the warmth texture of the dung
moisturizes and stays embedded until it becomes
another layer
For a while all is protected, but the built up
between the cow pies continues, bacteria after
bacteria fighting for dominance

The river is her savior, algae sips in

exposing the masters of the tootsies,
Her texturized hand creates a flood,
forcing enimies of flesh to seek deeper shelter,
The rough stone, scrubs, showing a never seen
polished maze of floors
Every massage tickles the veins uprooting the dead
dry skin, fresh soars blindly blinks, a heaven for
the leeches

Off she goes up the dust hill, the unknown awaits
all desparately searching for a new fresh home
The foot of the village girl

Quotes

"Satisfaction is a great deal achieved by a few."

"A relationship with a crack of a lie, is a balancing rock waiting for a bird drop."

"Two hearts can never be one without the loss of the other."

"A sizeable elephant roams with the bulls."

"The integrity of a broken man is a reflection of a trampled woman."

"Dedication and discipline clears up an obscured vision."

"You can not declare to know a man until you've experienced his presence in tranquility."

"A knowledgeable man suffers the most among scholars."

"Torch blowing a dying fire raises the flames."

Labour of love

Baby love, cry no more
light is upon you
It was out of love to lock you into that cave
It was for your own good to grow peacefully
for you are so precious to me
I chose darkness and isolation
You punished me terribly
Every morning I threw up
I craved for wild peas, so rare only pink
monkeys ate them
I devoured a rooster for breakfast
green tomatoes and okra were my enemies,
I loved you though, especially when you
made me crave for cakes

I loved you more when I felt your karate kicks
I loved you better when you gave me a fist bump
Every move you made was a sign of life
I fed you tons, a hippo was no match
You breathed the same breath as mine
Your pain I absorbed
You fought against the unknown
Your power punch destroyed them all
Your strong foot trampled them like ants
Countless days, weeks and months you
begged me to come out

I kept you in because I wanted you to grow
To come out a warrior, ready to take on the world
I felt your desperation but only I knew when it
was time
Well at least that's what I thought
Until you fought against my wishes

I felt the labour of love
Damn, your retribution, for loving you was harsh
The only offense I ever committed was
nurturing you
My crime was harboring and feeding my
own flesh
Finally after months of tough love
We made a pact, your freedom was
at last approved

What you had always desired and what
I had always wished
But for some reasons only known to you
you changed your mind
You went back on your word, you decided
to stay a little bit longer
I am your mother, I wasn't going
to allow any of that
Our relationship went from love to hurt
back to love, and then war
Crying, turned to screeching and scratching
groans of pain

You introduced yourself in spectacular fashion
For 12hrs you dictated the pace
You choked, grabbed and pulled the
walls of my womb
For 15hrs you wrestled until they
were about to cut me open
I screamed till my lungs gave way
I suffered violently, with a smirk on my face
but I did not give up on you, suddenly you
became tired

You wanted to make peace, but I didn't not
consent
For my battle had just begun
What I take in, I can take out

You gave me chills, frightened me, elevated my
mood
Plop, stuck, drop, you popped and I passed out
Not because you defeated me, no
I did it out of joy, out of my ever
loving love for you
You entered the world like a king, fist in
the air, ready for life's mission
And then you cried, yes you yelled
You cried for my warmness, for my touch
Oh it was a beautiful cry, a cry of freedom and
happiness

As soon as our eyes locked, I knew you
were mine for eternity.
Your chuckle blew me away, I will never
forget the day you were born, your love,
my love became our love
Be warned if you ever disrespect me,
disown me, hurt me in anyway
I will not hesitate to put you
back inside my womb,
He looked at me with watery eyes and
stuttered but it's too dark inside mummy

Abandoned

Big, bold and fearless
A thug of the kraal
The trough is mine
Green pastures, reserved all year
No movements until I move
No mooing till I roar

The head of the herd that follows,
They come in different colors and sizes, I
own all of you
The first to arrive the last to run
Survival is vital
Leaderless is death
Newcomers are welcome,
disobey, my horns are sharp, losing one hurts

What a hot day, rivers running dry
About to faint, heavily breathing snorting like a
cow
A hole in the sand, last drop to quench
My tongue in motion, for a deep slurp
A nudge fooled me
A quick look and the drink was gone

Unheard of and unseen
In a fit of rage, ready to strike
As my team watched
She burped and turned her back
Blinded and head over heels I followed like a
wimpy
Leaving everything behind to lead an unknown
herd.

Ms Perfectionist

As I sit I glow
Radiating perfection
Born to be Nr 1 Born to lead
Since birth I aim high

I don't compare I don't judge
I look up to me, I exalt thee

Fingernails manicured
Eyebrows blown
Lips ironed
Legs trimmed

Sharp brain
Sharp mind

When I lose I learn
When I pass I excel

I am never late, always on point
Distraction comes, destruct I do
My path is clear, little ones will follow
I am blessed, I work hard, I win
I love to love and to be loved
Never afraid of challenges
Mama taught me well
Although she left, in that short time,
accumulated wealth I did
Equiped with enough ammunition
A reinforced foundation
Been through it all,
Among familiar strangers I blossomed

Surrounded by hurt, envy and betrayal I overcame
As I catwalk, stomping on the wicked and evil
My blessings multiple
A life full of adventures
Loving what is not mine
Cheering for the opposite
Unkind hearts, plants without sunlight

Ms perfectionist is a brand
It's trending, become one, for you are loved

Tough Love

Tough love made me who I am today
I was raised up by my dad's eyes, fiery and
cunning. The coded signals detected the way
A cold stare meant don't even think about it
A side swipe, stop wasting my time
A decent conversation was a question after a
question
They were no rules, yet you could not break any
A thorough beating meant discipline of love
Failure was unacceptable
Impossible didnt exist
There is always a way was his theme

Past adulthood, love was formal
introduton, for approved couples
Relationships between children and parents was
respect and submission
Mother's love was through your stomach
Her gaze was your strength
When he roared with laughter the whole house
brightened up
There was never equal
He in front, mother behind
1st born followed by the 2nd born unless a son
was available, then he would have to skip the line.
Around the table papa feasted first, it was a good
feeling knowing you didnt need to initiate nothing,
If anything had to be done, it had to be done
prompt to perfection

The best was always expected of you, yet you were
never fully prepared for it, so was the nature of a

lion nurturing its cubs,
Touch one of us, the blows would rain down on
you
A feeling of love and respect cemented our family
Beaming with pride, dad would hold your hand
and all the long longed love would come rushing
back, reminiscence of a loving dad

Dip them

Inferior, curled in darkness
Living with fear and disappointment
Weather seasons passed on
No hope among the green trees
The bright sun, shines on all
Yet a gloomy cloud hovers above his head
A family he longed, a family he found
Scavenging was rearing

Around him they walked in stride, covered
in gold and pearls
Their skin glowed and their eyes sparkled
Laughter and joy a paradise on earth
Envy and cruelty flooded his mind

He wanted what they had, although there was
abundance
Sleeping became a pain as he skirmmed, seeked
and mingled with a dark power
Promises of riches and power excited him
Sacrifices and rituals didn't scare him
Soon he had assembled a clan, great minds think
alike, he assured them

Havoc and destruction engulfs the city
Murder and hate attracted the silent
Word spread, its either us or no one
Nobles and elites were paraded
Scholars and thinkers executed
Devil in one creates a thousand

Satisfied and jubilant tried to imitate the rulers,

indulged and rose in exellence
A child learns to be like his father
A stranger mimics the shadows

Halfway through, what is adopted cannot be real
Through piety and oppression the reins
began to slip
We outnumbered, they breed like fish
Dip them, cut them,
Fish smells
There is no end without a beginning

Dilemma

Along the aisle, nip picking, back eyes glaring
Bottom stuff out of reach, scarce at home
Legs jolting, limb stretching, fitness freak
Nonchalant, skin deep craving for a whistle
Shoe size, high heels, walk with style
Oldwine, age wise, a maturity cry

Born again, youthful feeling
Head high, lacking direction
Fooled once, took own course,
landed in a ditch
Swallowed hard, tried again
The world had moved

Met a couple, flocked together
Full of knowledge and laughter
Hope arose, face glowed
Instilled with new beauty
Delightful was the smile
A confidence of naivety

Friday came, skies opened
Adorned jewelry, and sweated in fragrance

As we rolled elegantly, a young bull stared
The crew nudged and I popped
Left eyed, fixiated on hind force
Missed on, all the shiny

Wanted to wrestle and choke

Rumpy pumpy Josh flushed, eyes lit
Murmured his name, spooking the invader
In the buff back broken
Dangled outside the pen
Made a call,
Lights off, slept in peace

Double Reflection

A spider web caught sight of me,
But I was not in the mirror, I saw a
reflection that wasn't mine
The mirror looked at me again, I hid and peeped
I was afraid of what the mirror saw in me
I was afraid of what I saw in the mirror
A cracked mirror suddenly became
squeak clean and full of light

It was no longer broken but full of life
A life that was not mine
A life I had not known
I was a stranger in my own being
A mirror that was not mine,
but the mirror told the truth
A truth that was not meant for me, but a
truth that was familiar

Behind me, a shadow, a shadow I didn't belong
too, a beautiful shadow
I wished the shadow could be me, clean cut,
perfectly dressed, a reflection of the man
that I longed to be,

Why should a shadow look better than me,
Is it a hidden message
Maybe I should listen, by the time I turned
I saw nothing but a broken glass, dripping with
redwine, shinning
with gold dust
A clear sign, go beyond what you deemed

Gone by 15

At 15years old, suddenly he awoke
A man, a boy in wonder
Childish dreams capitulated
Common faces vanished

A bull roaming among elephants
It was a strange feeling
Somehow like a twin, it knew him well
He walked without walking
Talked with his mouth closed

Visions directed his path
Some paved with joy,
others with doubtness
A vision told him otherwise
A body weak in strength, but bold in spirit

Easily angered, truthfully captivated
He rarely regretted, affection had deserted him
Saw only glory in his eyes
Never shy to say his mind
Superiors got intimidated, kept him in the fold
Not his way, was no way

Just like your grandpa, his mother yielded
He had focus, without descipline
A misguided missile destroys itself
By 30 he was back home, aged like his father

A glass short

Rich mouths served I rinsed
Treated as if a child
Protected and preserved
Kept cool out of reach taboo for
youngsters
Mild and bitter, sweet and sour
In the beginning there was calmness
soon followed by joy and sorrow
The devil in me is reserved for marathoners
Big, small, tall my wrath when provoked
has no mercy
They made me the way I am
Born out of a creative mind, clouded with
smoke and isolation
From the outside I look good,
quite charming, an attraction to the poison
I possess
They cheer and adulate, hoping I won't hurt them
laughter of delight. bringing out unknown
characters
In my midst the gentle survive
Ancestors rejoice and true colors are revealed
Don't dare do it under duress,
for I blend with anger
Organs bristle with joy, despise me,
yet they long for my presence
I keep them on their toes
A fight they are willing to take,
so long the grind continues
Disputes among ourselves breeds a new enermy
A mixture of toxins, disrupting the norm
why paint over a masterpiece
Mona Lisa and The scream are one hell of a drink

A good man

A stretched neck sees what no one else can see
No matter how inviting it seems, It is out of reach,
It's meant to tease my eyes, excite my nerves and
put my mind on a rollercoaster
I see lights blurring, stars exploding
My nostrils catch the aroma, blood drying on my
broken lips
The heavy load on my shoulders, bends my neck
Forcing me to stare down, blindness is
short sighted
Restricting the surge in my anxiety
My head antennas reactivate, strengthening my
neck muscles
Through the corner of my eye, coverd by a sweat
drop, a fly lays its eggs in my beard.
With my hands tied, I can shake and nod, the fly
tells me to be steady
As I drag my feet, years of burden,
a repetition I learnt from my fore fathers,
has turned me into a human machine
Carrying my own weight and ten others
born cursed, cause they sold out
I have never known peace, only their smiles
touch my heart
There are too young to understand, for them pain
and suffering is the way of the world
Wouldn't wish none of it on them, now I got to
break the barrier, I got to remove the curse, No
change comes without the loss of the past
Nothing new happens without the old dying out
Any sacrifice I make will free a generation to come
Too bad the worse I am in is the best I can do

Immigrant

Shunned from my motherland,
All hopes and dreams buried in a shallow grave
Proof of my life stamped and scribbled by the
highest honour
Through the grapevine all sail west,
Like sardines we are at the mercy of our captors,
Survival among eagle eyed scavengers, seeking a
part of you, so ruthless your soul gets lost in the
desert, being human means being hunted, for the
sake of another's life, no mercy, no remorse
their families await a served meal, only mother
nature feels your pain and if she is in a good mood,
she will lead your enermies astray and swallow
your children, either way you will have to endure
the pain. A pain of thirsty and hunger, for your
heart no longer seeks comfort.

Darkness becomes your saviour. Daylight, the
sand dunes buries your pitiless corpse, as deadly
scorpions hunt for a meal. By the time you reach
the mad sea, the walking dead rejoices.
One among them is always welcome, the
mysterious deep blue ruthless monster knows no
life. All are welcome but please allow me to drown
your souls. Your fate is mine, today I rejoice the
already buried mourn you
I will allow a few home, but not without showing
you my wrath, and swallowing a few baby souls,
Battering I will, cruxifying I shall, until your
return, I shall continue with my dominance, till
they dare not test me again.

Hey mama - mama mama mama oh oh oh,
hey papa - papa papa papa
I left without a word too ashmed to tell
Will you forgive me all I wanted was a better life
I never meant to leave broken hearts behind
My spirit has deserted me for my soul is wandering
why
Mama mama oh oh oh
Papa papa oh oh oh
Did I tell you how I got here
I walked
I ran
I swam
I jumped
My soul belongs in the wilderness I shall never no
peace until the curse is broken

"A silenced leader's gaze, stifles the oppressor."

"A shining star tainted by a dark spot discovers its superiority among stars."

"Why strike a match if lightning is within reach."

"A distinguished lady with a
stretched hand feeds a million."

"A leader without a vision is like an
antelope taking a drink in a crocodile
infested river."

"A rock formed from magma, cools
with wisdom and is filled with values
of life."

"A woman of class knows where
her beauty lies."

I still dream

He who guides me is who I follow
He who shines light on me is who I praise,
He who is there for me is who I respect,
Even though the anger in me lingers,
The anticipation never fades,
I hang on to a broken branch,
I cling on to a cracked wall,
My mind wanders, my eyes gazes,
I am well fed,
Well nurtured,
I am loved and showered,

Who can I blame, who am I to blame
For there is only one beautiful side,
The stigma stays, the scar reappears
Changing maybe with the season,
My moods, my tempers are notorious but
harmless yet unexplained,
My love, my kindness though given freely
are well measured, just in case
Why did it have to be like that,
Why me, But why at all,
The Vikings would say, that was the
will of the gods,
Well then, as hard as it is to accept,
sombre refills
Just as the sun is about to set,
a strange figure looms,
Singing praises with a feel and touch,
longed by my soul

In confusion, a solidified wall erupts, ready
to go to war with a distant voice

My own shadow, a slender figure shields
years of vengeance with a whisper,
a stroll and a soft touch
Out of darkness, white teeth grin, a smile
of the gods
The eyes dripping with calmness, a quick nod,
reassures war ready soldiers to stand down
Suddenly a cold sensation runs through my spine
A tear or two is what I cannot afford, back in my
mother's womb I curl
What is my own, feels strange,
A poke from the back, excites my soul
The shadow humbles, soft in nature
With a quick step I lunged, suddenly awoken a
dream I still dream, Daddy

Artificial Death

A happy family
Seeds of death sowed in between,
A successful husband blinded by the
limelight coughs in his sleep,
A professional with passion for health,
pricks her veins,
A vivacious teenage with love for life
succumbs under the bridge,
A heavily built boxer with a punch loses his jaw,
Suffering is the unknown seed,
sown dripping with the breath of the born dead

We used to tango, court, rejoice
Now sex is a deadly weapon,
We used to gather, drink, dance and laugh
Now our eyes are fixated on the wicked, seeking
revenge for a war created by the sick,
Love making was the ultimate pleasure,
Kissing and caressing
A flirt before marriage,
For centuries, ancient diseases
terminated the weak and the evil,
Nowadays a bold gallant knight heavily
protected falls due to a sniffle,

Death is no longer a curse, the masses
have become immuned,
Betting on who goes first,
No one knows where it came from,
A mysterious man in his modern cave
has just diluted his own,
Self inflicted, abundant wealth

No Greek dance the master and his
servants lay in anguish
Insulin the smell of death
Soon the elder will be extinguished
Planet covered by disfigured creatures
Until the cave man let us in, the big ballers are
destined for doom as the frail have already
perished

I came in blind

She was getting high from the weed she had smoked before and drunk from the alcohol she was consuming.

Dr. Neutrons knew his job well. It was like a bear falling on top of a rabbit and he foretold her of the pain to come.

She wandered what made elephants run so fast at short distances. She pictured the amount of sperm whales stored in their belly. She debated on whether she should have pleasure out of it or play dumb. He was not in the mood for fooling around.

His face had transformed into a scary creature. If she was to survive this encounter, then she needed to be in a different world. Her mind switched to the day, Teds plowed her plain thonged field. She remembered him smelling the grass, telling her it's gonna rain, she felt him feeling the texture of the leaking walls. He uprooted the bushes, and pulled the weeds out, whilst massaging the soil as the ground swelled up, bulging out, adjusting for a proper landing.

She observed him plant his seeds and sprinkled the plants. She felt the roots sprouting, spreading into every vein. It was glorious and satisfying. Her damp body became slippery and flooded. The spirited captured soldiers were quickly flushed into oblivion.

She smiled slyly at the seemingly inevitable victory but only to be flipped over violently. Her vision switched to Graeme. That dude could make it rain like a Waterfall.

She remembered Ted threatening her, "if you ever touch that Waterfall guy again, I am going to snap your neck out." She was becoming a bit hazy and more like in a vegetative state. She needed reinforcement. Her spirit of MaMoyo, her totem was dying to be unleashed, to seek vengeance. Her eyes popped out as if her nipples had been electrocuted. Masibanda was scuffling with MaMoyo, squeezing each other's breath out. They had awoken up the beast of Mutare, and provoked the ghost of Mutoko. These spirits were now free to roam and they were on a roll. She had summoned and commanded, the souls of her ancestors, gran of her grannies.

As he desperately tried to fathom the ocean and tear her into pieces, his eyes suddenly bolted out. He choked and froze. His back stiffened, as the shadows of the unknown warriors hovered above him. Lifting the heavy burden, off her cursed back. She watched her soul stare awkwardly at the old fighting bear, losing what it thought was an easy meal. As he struggled to run uphill, almost snapping the foot of a mountain goat, he winced and stumbled, fell on his back, rolled over, hunger and thirst in his eyes, as its meal invitingly lay in wait. Out of breath, out of strength, eyes glowing, and snarling like a dog refusing to back off, he clutched her ankle with his paws. Not willing to give up, she mewed like a cat and smiled.

"You think you can come into my house, brutalize me, pummel and abuse me. Well I am gifted and a step ahead of you. I know each and every corner of my oasis, my weapons are invisible, hidden in every sac and are very effective. When I start fighting back, you better be at your best," she bragged about herself.

New energy and power flew into her body. She poked him cautiously like a dead lion, waiting for a sign of life.

"You got no idea who I am old man," she downed the rest of her cognac and did a libation, celebrating victory with her ancestors. She pulled a cigarette and made smoke rings while lying on her back with her knees up.

"Yeah I have faced similar foes before, ask Ted and Graeme, tied them ass up, beat that one," she silently propped herself, seeking assurance.

For some reason her surroundings had become battle grounds.

"You wanna listen to my heartbeat," she chuckled.

He grinned and wormed himself towards her. After what seemed like an eternity, he got up and blended some juice.

“A croc is a gourmet, doesn’t
digest in one go.”

“At 1000 km/h a flightless bird will
never taste airborne.”

“Unnecessary empty rhetoric and
gibberish diminishes value and casts a
shadow over beautifulness.”

"A genuinely loving woman knows no other."

""In the dark every shadow is mysterious."

Tell it to her

When you walk, the birds whistle and bow
Your body is a magician's trick, twisted
and curved, a sculptor's dream
Look at those arms, long, and smooth
When you raise them the wind breezes
Your palms a texture of velvet,
Queen Elizabeth would applause

I will not talk about the eyes, round and big,
Brown and mesmerizing
Watery and teasing, an apple will fall
Oh I love them, they can see through
my pure heart

With you it never pours, rain comes in drops,
afraid it might spoil your long mermaid hair
When you breathe, your body shakes causing
earth quakes in paradise

I love those thick lips, my permanent
chocolate, oh, a child in a factory
After the Lord our God, you are the 2nd
wonder of the world
So pure, so wonderful, nature's first call,
when disaster is imminent
If I have to die, a glimpse of you, will
make death a wish

Only if you could be mine, I would turn
a bunch of twigs into a fountain of roses
I would create a star that shines wherever you
walk

I would give you love and laughter
When you cough diamonds spill
Thank you for your beauty and kindness,
A man like me
I can only savour in a trail of air that
you leave behind
Go well beauty queen, after a few bottles,
courage will follow

Craving

The alleys of death,
Smeared with hunger and evil
Dodging and diving, escaping the law
Made a scapegoat coz my will is lit
Back home, dad's ego is high
I got to run, every move is a scorn

Family is blood, I roam with thugs
My mind is blank, hate is all I see
Born with a bone, ribs I crack
Save my soul, scalps decay

No remorse, I take yours for good
Roaches I roast, blinks blinds the weak
Panda footed, wishing for double shells
Death is ready, life is a show

Shadows scare, in darkness I breathe
Feeding on tequilas, a mean look is a killer
Losing my life, props forever
For we aim for the top, hills are mined
Cowering dirty and low, a miss is a maim

The life I have, the dead spurn
Diamond is the shape, a lid I close

Tears for a child

Your smile is like candy
Your teeth are like cream

Can you see me
No you cannot, but I can feel your breath
You little eyes are full of questions
Questions you don't understand
Think no further, for you are in the wilderness
In the wilderness the strong, the wild, and
the you, survive

Waste no fear, for I am closer that you think
I wish it could be different,
But there is no difference,
I am you, and you are me
No matter what

They will try to fill you with nonsense
It's expected, because they are full of nonsense
They don't know, no better,
Forgive them, when the time comes
They will cry
Tears of blood
Tears of sorrow
They will plead and beg

We are at peace, for no vengeance was in play
Watch their faces fold, and overlap
Misery they look
We are dumbfounded
For only love exists between us
Sometimes I wish I could cry

But your strength, forbids me
You are destined for greatness
Without greatness, I am only a father

I did not wish for this
I did not decide this
I did not force this
I did not want this

Your life
Your soul
Your heart
Your face
Yes I made you
Yes I miss you

But why
You could have been right here with me
You could have learnt everything from me
My culture
My language
My beliefs
My character

We roam with lions
Weakness is forbidden
Cries are taboo

Now you are all grown, consumed with confusion
None of it was my making,
None was my wish
But all is my fault

A father's blood is a son's life
I will not judge anyone, and you shall
not judge nobody
Be grateful you resemble your grandfather,
Your blood ancestral, filled with ancestral love

You are never alone
Just breathe deeply, and the world is yours
No excuses, don't blame your mother
You are bigger than your nose

Shades of affiliation

There was a great rift between the two great guardians of the African continent. After centuries of abusing women. The mermen were banished from venturing outside the waters.
When peace was finally restored kojo was rejected by both parties. He worked tirelessly whenever his services were called upon but he was never fully trusted by anyone, since he was half of both worlds. He became a lost soul and wandered in the wilderness, offering his wicked expertise to whoever desired them. As he crouched eagerly in one of the tallest trees, listening to the menacing moanings of the immortal beings, baying for vengeance.

His eyes crossed, becoming pure white, a flurry of flash backs exploded in his head. He saw a beautiful young girl with a group of other girls going to fetch water in a local river. As they filled their buckets, a decorated merman hiding in the water behind some shrubs became attracted to this young girl.
The merman concentrated his eyes on her and she nearly fell into the water as she responded to his call but the other grils held her back. In the process of helping her, she dropped her wrist band into the water. The merman came to the edge of the river and watched her salaciously as she returned to the village.

In the middle of the night whilst the girl was sleeping, the merman used the wrist band to wake her up telepathically. She got up half naked and followed his mesmerizing voice back to the river.

She walked in the darkness as if she was awake. At the river she removed her clothes and lay down by the grass. The massive merman crawled out with a strong sexual desire, and moaned the whole night as he made love to her. When it was dawn she suddenly awoke not knowing were she was. She gathered her clothing and ran back home.

The merman somersaulted a couple times and disappeared underwater. Each night the merman would lure her to the river and make love to her. One particular night as she was returning home, her father was about to come out of the latrine when he noticed her almost naked. He hid himself and wandered. He was greatly troubled. She was his only daughter. That following night he did not sleep. When he heard the door squeaking he armed himself with a spear.

He silently foreshadowed her before realizing she was under some kind of a spell. He observed her performing the same ritual. As she lay on the ground a giant of a merman stood out of the water and threw himself on top of her. The father angry and shaken ran out of the bush holding his spear high ready to kill. Just as he was about to thrust the spear through his back, he turned around and shrieked. The old man hesitated but the love of his daughter gave him courage and pierced the spear through his abdomen.
The merman screeched in pain and threw the old man into the river. The old man sprung up, striking

him, and taking away part of his ear. The young girl suddenly awoke just as the merman was jumping for the father ready to take away his life.

She screamed in horror. The merman was distracted. He pulled out the spear out of his stomach and was about to kill the old man. Then he paused and stared at her. The look in her eyes mellowed the merman's heart. He threw the spear away and dragged the father underwater.

The young girl ran home to call for help but the father was never seen again. Rumors circulated in the village that she was having an affair with the father and were caught in an uncompromising position, that's why the mermen took him.

The village shunned her and she endured animosity from the locals. She ran away from home when she discovered she was pregnant. She had caused her mother enough pain already. For months she travelled with a group of nomads.

One night as she slept under a tree, next to a small fire, she was awoken by heavy raining and thunderstorms, that's when her water broke.

The nomads held her down and tried to assist her. She was bleeding and was in excruciating pain for hours, screaming and shouting.

Finally the baby popped out into the hands of an elder nomad. But he quickly threw it to the ground, when he noticed the baby had no legs but a fin. They all scattered in fear.

The baby wiggled nervously in the rain. The

nomads mumbled in prayer, asking for protection and forgiveness. A hyena distracted them, made a creepy sound, laughing as it came out of nowhere and bit the fin, dragging it into the dark. The nomads out of fear threw their spears and killed it. The baby in shock sprung up and the fin broke. A young boy with evil tubular eyes and big lens stood in front of them struggling for breath.

The nomads terrified, ran for cover, they had never witnessed such a scary miracle. The young boy with such quickness chased after them in the dark. There was brutal beatings and growling as the nomads cried for help. The hapless young girl lay helpless on the ground too weak to move. She had lost a lot of blood, and she was about to lose consciousness.

The young boy appeared holding four human heads. He threw them at the mother, his body covered in blood.

She struggled to speak, "Kojo, Kojo," and she passed out. He shrieked, his cry echoing far and wide, deep and wrenching.

The water spirits heard the cry and they knew a powerful curse had been cast. Mama Oyiwas from deep underneath the ocean directed a lightning to struck him down.

The immortal spirits filled with anger observed him from within their shadows. The lightning missed him by inches as Aragognto Paradza the immortal warrior intervened, pushing him aside. Kojo frightened and spooked limped off, disappearing into the night leaving his mother to die.

Python tales

Coiled within a striking distance
Trajectory, a millimeter an hour
Every nerve is activated, a meal on my mind
You look simple no weapons visible, if I get
closer my prayers have been answered
A feed a day, a season to last

Patience is a virtue, two holes you are gone
Tough skin, shiny spots, a fool's rose
Tainted milk is not for the faint hearted
The heavier the slower, the tighter the grip
My condelences your body is mine, tailored to
perfection

A bit I feel, till you beat no more
As we cross eyes I pour my love on you,
A kiss on the forehead, your last blink tells
me you drowsy
I fine tune my jaws, flexibility is an art
My tactics are secrect but I make you watch,
for you swore to die with them
I wish I could undress you, cotton and
rubber nauseate me

Your bones create a melody, let it last a bit longer
Done this a couple of times, somehow
you are different
It's a habit I need to feed, without you
an empty stomach rumbles
I did warn you, curiosity mesmerized your gaze
The last one was huge, bones as soft as jelly
Squeezed too tight, burst open all juices lost

I learnt, Pore Pore, it's a rythm that
suits all
At least you have no babies like that crazy warthog
They bit me till I escaped

Here comes the easiest part,
It's head in and the rest follows
What a miracle, within a short time
I have just gained a few pounds
My movements are slow
I have to hide in case they come searching
Thank you for the warmth
The taste comes later
Until we meet again
You will always be safe inside me

Adopted life

Slap slap slap slap
He has a hold on me
His tentacles spread far and wide
For every new born, the umblical cord is his
The world is a mirror ball
A game of his, all arrows
point to disaster
With a single cough, millions will sneeze

Before birth your fate is decided
A great deceiver
With a tongue coated in honey
The power is his wealth
His strength is your brain
For manipulation is a division symbol that
multiplies hate,

A grin with a blitz
An eye with no shame

Greediness and cruelty
A challenge for his siblings
None are born stoned
Courtesy of the elder
The young learn fast
The process is perfected
Doomed to fail
A last bite, he cries out

Quotes

*"Tread cautiously a well planned trip,
loosens the lips."*

"A loved one with faults kills the spark."

Trader's worship

I believe our beliefs are from the higher power
You might not know me
I am from a land where grass doesn't grow
Far away, beyond the sacred mountains
We grew up as cattle herders
Born full of pride like your tribe
We had nothing except our spirit
Look where we are now
We roam the streets, King Solomon's gold
is what we have
When we walk elephants jostle to watch
I am a lion, not just a lion, the one that
eats other lions
I am a generous lion, that feeds
and saves some for our brethren
Sharing is what we do
You walk in our pride, you are forever part of us
We might migrate, wherever we go, you name will
be sang out loud
My missus next to me will fulfill our pact
Incase I don't make it
Her nod is my word
You see, we are forever bonded
I give
You take
You stamp
By my side, your children will not starve
Remove the curse of povert
Your mistakes, can be easily rectfied
That diamond ring, that sparkles in your
wife's eye
Got two in the boot

Be open minded
Innocence and cleverness go hand in hand
Your eyes tell me, you are a born winner
I can elevate you
Use me as a spring board and achieve
greatness at my expense
Act fast
No one is looking
Your pocket is my pocket
An overall has deeper holes

They call me SHUMBA MHAZI a powerful totem
not matched by many

My brethren I did not jump the que by mistake
Your soul searched for me
Four truck loads in wait
Clearance is your proffession
This is your home
Walk we shall, along the Beitgridge
Just relax, Limpopo got eyes

Before I depart

Two souls, hopeful in anguish
Strange tongues, they spoke
Battling on two fronts
Expandable gazes of wrath
Caught in the same net
Bubbles of life slowly escaping

They wriggled for freedom
Pushed towards each other' s arms
So close they come
So close they parted
A fingertip away
Slowly they drifted

I never knew you
Yes I stuck close to home
You are not one of us
A shoal don't mingle
Your stare of awe or famished
Two opposites, none can escape, hunger
not on my mind

A journey they didn't choose
Now destined to feed a household

A fate we share
A friendly hug, won't hurt a bug,
before I depart

The door

There is no turning back
Forces of will, lay in wait
Your deeds no one else
You cross that line,
on your own, you shall enter

Beyond your wisdom, riots of salvation,
chaos of liberation
Deliverance will be free
Ransom of gold
The meek will prosper

Step away, immunity I grant
A relief I discharge
The privileged have a day off
Free pass if you can recite

Morning Prayer

My ladylove, inamorata
Wooer of my desires
Extinquisher of my flames
Loyal, kind a craving for my heart
Faithful and humble a man's dream

You are spiritually adored
Affectionately absorbed
Generous and passionate a natural
hobby you posses

Sympathetic, cheerful a fond hand I offer
My pastime, caring and loving
Warmheartedness a courtesy I adopted

I rest in your presence, full of grace and sweetness
Wish you a spotless day
Uchi wangu (my honey)
My ladylove, inamorata

Last Hope

It was midday, the sky was blue, and the sun was smiling brightly. They drove through a cluster of dilapidated huts. The dusty, donkey-drawn road had never seen a car before, it was bumpy and narrow. Freddy did not say a word, he looked nervous, and that made Moritz and Boris worry.
At the end of the road, they took a sharp turn and followed a dry stream that led to a stone canal. The canal ended abruptly and green vegetation sprawled across an arm of the sea. Mountains stood on the side, silently encompassed by barren land full of sand and stones.
A huge tree stood guard into an opening that appeared at the edge of the mountain. Freddy sighed heavily and stopped the car. "We have to walk the rest of the way. Please leave your phones, no gadgets, no cameras. If you have anything to say, say it now. As soon as we make the first step, no talking, it's disrespectful to the spirits." He spoke with a firm voice Moritz, and Boris sensed his intensity and nodded their heads.
They folded their trousers to their knees and walked barefooted across the rugged surface. In the distance, a drumbeat rhythmically, warning of incoming intruders. When they reached the edge of the compound, a strong foul smell blew into their faces.
The sound of the drumbeat became louder and louder. They sneezed and coughed, inhaling the stench. Moritz and Boris suddenly became agitated. Their hairs stood, and their knees trembled.
They wanted to scream, but their voices had

deserted them. Freddy staggered forward with a death stare on his face.

They maneuvered along a tiny two lane strip paved with python skins and skeletons of scary creatures. There was glittering oil sprinkled on portions of the skins. Jars filled with liquids, organs, and dead animals lined the pathway. A gigantic crocodile skull hung above the entrance, which was decorated by strange animal skulls. There were hundreds of dead monkey feet, pangolin scales, and tails of a hyena.

They crossed a white and red piece of cloth, laid midway. And as if possessed, and in a trance, they began to jiggle to the beat. From inside, six pairs of ghostlike images watched and marked them like hunted animals.

They shook, and wiggled for hours until they were in their undergarments. A mysterious dark Blanket of smoke enveloped the area. The clouds, stars, and the moon seized to exist. A sharp faster drumbeat took over, and three skinny half-naked men with white painted faces emerged. They blindfolded them and put a noose around their necks, dragging them inside. Trickles of water fell on their heads. They led them through dungeons and halls of caves. Sharp stones bruised their feet. They walked up and down, deeper into the mountain and across streams of water. They stood for a while in a room blistering with heat. Someone pushed their knees down and removed the blindfolds.

They found themselves kneeling in front of Nganga. The place was surprisingly clean, brightly lit, and a semi-circle shrine stood behind neatly arranged. They were skulls of weird creatures staring at them.

Nganga was a young man dressed in a pristine red shirt. The three men were not convinced but were afraid to talk for fear of losing their voices. Nganga quickly got up and smiled at something behind them. He threw some white powder in the air, and in anticipation they turned their heads. A shadow flew above them, creating a trail of dust. An old Nganga wearing stripes of wild animals skins appeared. He had feathers of birds on his head. He wore various ornaments of crocodile, lion, leopard, and squirrel teeth around his neck. Beads and rattling seedpods covered his arms and legs. His face and body had red and white markings. In the middle of his white afro hair, a chicken foot was perfectly tucked in.

Without paying any attention to his guests, he squatted opposite them and started playing dice with some bones. He mumbled and chattered to himself as he threw tiny bones on a mat. He fell back screaming, fear on his face.
Moritz, Boris, and Freddy followed his movements with their wide eyes.
"Muyedzo don't just stand there, give the visitors food and beer to drink and eat." He spoke english fluently. The men contradicted themselves and shook their heads. Nganga was not pleased with their gestures. He sprung up to his feet and lectured them.

"How dare you deny my ancestors." He screamed and spat on the floor. His voice became deeper and inaudible.

"Ninyi vyura wadogo watatu, mnaingia nyumbani kwa Sangoma na kukataa kula chakula chake. Huna heshima, ninapaswa kukugeuza kuwa kobe."

(You three little frogs, you come into Nganga's house and refuse to eat his food. You have no respect, I should turn you into tortoises)

He took out some polished bones inside a headless fish and threw them on the ground. A bonfire erupted in the middle of the room touching the top of the ceiling, and immediately simmered.

Muyedzo hurriedly saved them whilst disparaging them.
"I want to warn you. Don't you dare to disrespect Sekuru, eat your food immediately before he gets angry."
He placed down two big tortoise shells crammed with meat and sima and a hairy horn filled with a milky drink. The three men ate and drank like hungry lions. Consumed in the tasty of the food, Nganga yelled.
"Je! Ni kuzimu gani, hiyo ilitokeaje, sijawahi kuona kitu kama hiki hapo awali."
(What the hell, how did that happen? I have never seen anything like this before.)

They stopped grazing and gawked at him. He lifted
his head, with an intimidating look on his face.
Somehow he was not convinced, he sprinkled
some liquid and cupped the bones and blew into
them. He slowly threw them again as if expecting a
different result. With his heart thudding fast, he
muttered, and communicated with the still bones.
The bones shimmered, reflecting a dull light, and
blood appeared on one of them. Nganga stumbled
and clasped his hands, visibly shocked. Drumbeats
suddenly filled the room. Three young women
covered in colorful material jumped in the middle,
and the place became a pulsating, frenzied dance
area. The women were erratically hopping, shaking,
and ululating, in a circle. They danced for hours
nonstop. Meanwhile, Nganga lay back, his eyes
wide open, his body jerking. He looked as if he had
entered a spiritual realm.

The men tucked themselves in a corner and
observed science in the making. A gust of wind
swirled, levitating Nganga. The dance floor cleared,
and the drumbeats reduced to a light tapping sound.
A spiritual voice of authority echoed.
Nganga was unconscious, levitated in the air.

*"Kusahau kuhusu Vera, bado yuko hai, lakini sio muda
mrefu. Wengi wanatamani damu yake. Dhambi za maba-
bu zake. Yeye hataonekana tena, milele."*

(Forget about Vera she is still alive, but not for long.
Many crave her blood. The sins of her ancestors.

She will never be seen again, forever.)

After the words were spoken, Nganga fell to the ground. A cold, burning fog filled the room. Freddy, Moritz, and Boris staggered out of the cave, almost naked.
They found their clothes thrown on the ground with small pyramids of stones next to them. They looked as if they had just walked out of an all-night party. No one said a word. What they had just witnessed and heard was unfathomable. Their beliefs, perceptions, and cultural values were hijacked and scorched.
Boris trembled with fear. Moritz was awe stricken, he was experiencing a change of energy. He had been cleansed and somehow longed for more. Freddy strode in front, pretending to have handled it accordingly. They walked in silence, and when they had reached a certain point, a fresh breeze woke them. That is when they realized they were naked. They hastily put on their clothes and walked as fast as they could towards where they had parked the car. Strangely, they seemed to have bypassed the place. A long narrow path covered with dried cow dung appeared from nowhere. There was no sign of the car. Boris began to sob. He was too overwhelmed. No one cared to soothe him. The previous events had touched a nerve.

They walked along the path without saying a word until a young boy in cattle drawn cart gave them a ride.

"I should never have gone there, I will never be the same again. I see ghosts, ghosts, everywhere." Boris mumbled.

When they got to the camp the jeep was parked next to Moritz's hut. They gasped but nothing seemed strange anymore. Freddy warned them not to talk about it for the next three days or else they would go mad.

63

"A human being with a choice creates circumstances"

"A jumping baby is a happy man."

"Pre existing assumptions triggered by unconscious bias, justifies the cultural homogeneity of our society."

"*Destiny is a word designed to limit your expectations.*"

"*Dedication and discipline clears up an obscured vision.*"

"*A genuinely loving woman knows no other.*"

Misfortune

Hapless befell the wicked
Disaster strike the evil
Misery affects the weak
Suffering is for non believers

Rich in wealth
Rich in health
Rich in life
Richness lies in you

Kill for ill gains
Destroy for indulgence
Structures dismantled
A one way road need no directions

Ruthless in being, criminals for hire
Mobs on standby
A simple man wants to be a king

Selfish they come
Dine and wine, imposters of doom
Dressed regal, hellfire need no fuel
Baptism will prevail

Stillborn

A twin in me
twenty years youger
A twin of a kind
Fought battles with giants of nature
Frail and helpless
A war I felt,
A fight he fought with unknown
enemies, vying for his breath
A mother's greatest pain, is watching her own sink

Taken away
Removed
before his time
Deliverance came way too soon ,
A battle in defeat, a battle he won
No love lost your soul stays with me
for a broken heart dares the darkness
double we shall be judged
Farewell
you dodged the pain
you cheated death
angels don't die
nor are they born
A speedy journey
in heaven they will rejoice

Take a plunge

Eligible, unattached, available
Gear up, take a plunge
Join the aisle of joy
Be exalted and euphoric
Tie the knot,
Take a beauty to the alter
A committment your heart knows

Charmed angels with matching
wings have already assembled
Gold, silver wear line up the tables

She is not only a wife
but a friend, a soulmate untill the end of your days
I am well grounded, enlightened
I learnt from the wiseman
Love, love is for courting
Devotion, light up the flames
No weak knees, your fate has been sealed

Spiritual protection is needed, in
human form a gator can be charming
Choose wisely, tame your needs and
inspire a generation
Celibatist is a curse for a lone woman
Take a plunge

Sparrow

I am the tiniest and the bravest
My bones are hard as nails
I feed on the best there is to find
The first to arise, the last to rally
Any slightest movement I shuck and jive
Night hunters chase me, day gatherers flourish
My crew relies on my instincts
If I slip, one of us goes missing

The gang is aware of our codes
Slow in reaction, your life span is short
There are days I like to sing, knowing fully
well I am exposing myself
The joy of being heard and entertaining
nature overcomes me
Sitting ontop of the tallest, I let my voice fly
Soon others join, forgetting the dangers around us
In the midst of fun, one voice is silenced
Scattering in different directions, some are lost
forever
On your own life can be miserable
Wherever we go, we are watched, trapped, enticed
In numbers we decrease, in birth we multiply
To be hunted is the universal way, but you cannot
silence a sparrow

A farmer' dilemma

Multiple strokes, a beatdown body,
luxury is a nap
Each pain a reminder to keep on labouring
My time on this planet is slowly nearing
Its been a long journey, more
accomplishments linger
To tell it to the youth, with laughter they applaud
I was the third generation the last still standing
Minds are busy absorbed with news
A world leaving nature in ruin
At the end of the fields babies are chosen
Some are devoured, wild times even
animals make choices
A barren land missing a sprout, hard
times ahead Families are dismantled

Skin as rugged as the dry soil, a trace of my steps
Born with two hands turned into shovels,
nothing matches the effort in me
Despite, marching continues, dragging feet,
a trail of struggle
From earth we shall live, as long as
the dust settles in peace
Familiar territory, dry winds mean no rain
Deep down sixty feet under, tunnels
of water guggle, too long to quench our thirsty

Prayers of rain, prayers of fortune,
sparrows still fly
Hundred heads behind me, good times did exist
A legacy you leave, out of all some will crack
A lady with a streched hand, begging is not an

option but it is what they seek
Cannot blame them, gorged eyes and dry
lips, a sign, food is scarce
Keep your head low, even the wise get stuck
Miracles do occur, the feel though, strangles hope
Logicall thinking, it's time to pack and go
Technically focused, hidden gems are in plain sight
What we strive for is a step away, blindness ruin
our vision

Childhood friends

When we were kids
We fell for each other

A group of boys wanting nothing other than fun
Our talks where childish homour
True believers of what we thought
Collaborators paid with open palms
Life was great then till we had to grow

Our minds opened up, our eyes started rolling
Adolescene a struggle to fit
What was in front of us suddenly was a talking
point
Our ways changed, our looks became a passion
Offering a helping hand to strangers, to
please teens who didn't care
Duties started flying in, responsibility a
must if you wanted to live to see another day

As we grew up, consumed with a new world
Our tales took a different turn
Our bodies reacted without authorisation
The bond was still strong, immaturities creeped in
Some fell off, some grew too fast
Thrown to the wolves, mature beyond our years
Fully aware of our needs, challenges awoke us
Alone in a battlefield, surrounded by charmers and
snake handlers
A quick adjustment, no loss is too small
The chasers stood idle, watching our level harness
and tame the ripened

The world has four stages, a master
of all has no patience
In the deep end we divided, among the
sharks we progressed
Perfected the game, learnt to see clearly
Outgrown the rest, indecence took root
A bull without a scar, is a steer with venom
Escaped by whiskers, turned a new leaf
Thrived in life, so did my homies

Back together again
Looking behind, a kid in front, reminds
me of myself
Happy that we still friends, our children
can chill while we gracefully age

"Lazy dreamers are the best, their dreams never end."

"Destiny is a word designed to limit your expectations."

"Unnecessary empty rhetoric and gibberish diminishes value and casts a shadow over beautifulness."

Quotes

"A distinguished lady with a stretched hand feeds a million."

"Don't ever underestimate a man with a plan."

"Scattered seeds weakens the bond."

"Repeated slave shows, heats up a mild nostalgia and weaponizes a nefarious mind."

She was now basically a prisoner, she could not go to school and if she did she would have to wait for hours before he came back.

At one point she was forced to sit the whole night with old drunk men in a 24-hour bar. Her disdain and hatred for him grew each day. She could only leave the house with him and was forced to follow him wherever he went. He would park the car and leave her sitting inside for hours.

Many times the car got close to being towed away. Whenever she went looking for him. He would be gambling in hidden betting shops close by.

The time to renew her visa came, they asked her to bring an attendance confirmation from the school, her Anmeldung, to confirm her address and her bank statement, to show that she had the 8,000 euros in her account. She had none of those and she knew she had hit a barrier.

When she got home around 4 pm Marko was nowhere to be found and he was not picking up his calls.

She checked his friends's Facebook accounts and noticed one of them had posted about wanting to attend a party that day.

She went and sat in a hotel bar so she could use the internet and keep herself warm.

She bought a liter of water, some bread rolls and

a small bottle of Jägermeister from the supermarket, since hotel prices were too high. Her attire was not for partying and she wondered if they would let her in the club. She had made up her mind that this would be the last time he would ever disrespect her ever again.

She prayed that she would find him in that club and that she would hurt him badly. Around midnight she chatted up some guys and they helped her sneak into the club. She was tipsy and drunk with anger. He had shown his disregard for her and she had nothing to lose anymore. She just wanted to hurt him, break his leg or stab him. She lay in waiting, hidden in a dark corner, where she could see who came in and who went out without her being noticed. As she observed the entrance she started having seconds thoughts.

If the police where called and she was caught she could be deported. She had two choices either she was going to accept being treated like a slave or swallow her pride and stomp his head

She decided to put an end to it. And putting a stop to it meant intimidating him, instilling fear in him like BJ had said. Around 3 am she was almost giving up when Dino walked in with 2 girls, one of them was Sonia, Marko's baby mama.

"Bitch sold me out," she snarled. A couple of minutes later Marko joined them. She sat there waiting for

them to be comfortable. Her bottle of Jägermeister was almost empty, she grabbed an unattended half-full bottle of beer from the table and drank it.
She was high and full of anger. Alcohol and anger are the worst enemies. She observed them with an intensity of a lion preying on Zebra. She was like a soldier sneaking on her enemies. As she marched towards Marko and his crew, somehow Dino spotted her. He ran to warn his friend.
Marko was startled, he got up and charged towards her. He thought he could scare her away, but Chipo was determined.

She was gnarling, hissing and clawing, people thought she was mad. Marko smiled as he approached her as if nothing had happened. He raised his arms about to hug her. She whacked his head with the beer bottle, He was caught by surprise, blood splattered on his pristine white ironed shirt. He sprung at her as she was about to strike again. He tried to choke her but she dodged. Marko was taken aback by her speed. As she swung again Dino jumped in and blocked the 2nd strike. Dino's big body saved Marko from further beatings but he took all the punches.
"Hey, Marko, this is embarrassing man, take your woman home, take her home, we don't roll like this man," Dino shouted. The crowd started to gather

around them. The DJ stopped playing music and the security was approaching fast. The women in the club were looking at her in shock, they had never seen such violence.

"Wow I wonder what he did to her," someone from the crowed yelled.

"Hey let her go she is a woman, you cheater, fight with your own size, asshole," shouted some girls.

She was surging forward, desperately wanting to batter and whack him more. It was as if a giant scorpion was fighting with both hands and feet. As she attempted to crawl on him the hulk security guard picked them up like toys. They were thrown out of the club. She was still seething with anger. Dino was holding her from behind, as Marko wobbled a safe distance towards the car. She was dragged inside the car full of anger and was uncontrollable. Marko on the other hand was hysterical, a raging bull. He kept hitting the steering wheel promising her that he would end her life that night.

He drove so fast like Lewis Hamilton and was as erratic as Verstappen. All the while he was punching the dash board and going through red traffic lights. He was cursing and fuming, giving her that dirty look, that murderous stare. Dino sat in front but kept his eye on her.

He was ready to prevent her from throwing any

punches. He was a busy man that night. And she was not backing down.

"You have messed up with the wrong woman, I am from Zimbabwe and I will deal with you, I am gonna murder your ass." She screamed at him.
"What, me?"
He braked suddenly, the car screeched and stopped in the middle of the bridge. He went around the car and pulled the door open. Blows began raining, it was blows for blows. He dragged her out, tried to lift her up, wanting to throw her over the bridge. Dino tackled them both to the ground.
Chipo found herself free, she ran back to the car and took a jack from underneath the seat, as Marko approached in full speed from behind, she swung, slamming the jack right into his face and he fell to the ground. Dino froze in shock, he was stunned. Blood spattered over his face. "Unoda kuita zveku-tamba neni, handisi mwana wamai vako, nhasi ndo-kuuraya."
(Don't mess around with me, I am not your mother's child, I am going to kill you today)

"Shit this bitch is crazy yo!" Dino yelled. "The poli-ce will be here any minute Marko, if you don't con-trol yourself, this means jail man, you know what I mean. Let's get out of here man."

Marko lay there for a few minutes his eyes wide open. "Are you okay buddy? Get up we need to go before we get arrested. Give me the keys, let me drive."

"No I am good," he shouted as he got up.

"Are you sure homie, you wanna drive," Dino asked again, looking worried.

"Damn, I am gonna kill this crazy bitch," Marko screamed hitting the steering wheel. He struggled to put the key in the ignition.

"Are you concussed."

Marco stared ahead for a while and shook his head. He took off at top speed, he was driving wayward, totally out of control. As they came around McDonald's, he slowed down to turn into the road that led to their apartment.

He seemed to have recovered, out of anger and frustration of being beaten by a woman, he threw a beer bottle, that caught Chipo by surpised. It hit her on the forehead. It shook her and with animal instincts she forcefully thrusted her leg out, and caught Dino by mistake who slumped onto Marko causing the car to swerve and hit a pavement, taking out a few bicycles in the way. She plunged for his neck and choked him against the headrest from behind.

"Hey, stop, stop you will kill him, this is not good," Dino was shouting nervously. He got out and desperately tried to pull her out of the car.

"I will fucken eviscerate you, I will skin you alive, you don't get to disrespect me like that."

She screamed as she struggled with Dino. "This shit gotta stop man, let's chill man, relax people," Dino was in panic mode.

"We will have the police all over us man," he was trying not to yell.

"Come princess let me take you home, we can talk about it tomorrow," he begged her, as he dragged her away. All the time Dino was observing the streets, looking around to see if no one had seen them. And for once Chipo saw fear in Marko's eyes, he knew he had messed with the wrong person.

Chipo wanted to inflict as much pain on him as possible. Marko knew his image had been tarnished, but he was arrogant, he wasn't going to let a chick slap him around.

"I want you out of my house, you ungrateful bitch." He shouted after them, blood running from his nose.

"Come and get some more," she yelled back.

Dino had to force her into the house. "Look here, what you are doing is too dangerous for you, if the police come, you will be in big trouble. You know what I mean. You have made your point, so chill. Marko is terrified of you, I have never seen him like that. Let's talk about it tomorrow," He pleaded with her and tried to calm her down.

A mother's love can be a curse

One and only stood tall and loved
Attached to one, confused by the other
Success was always the goal, a level too far to
attain
Hustled and tusseled one had to survive
With discipline and focus I shredded through the
crowd
Guided by an unknown force, a choice not mine
Wherever the wind blew, my nostrils smelt gold
Shadows and whispers were just background noise
Finally reached the top, amassed abundant wealth
still I lacked
Kept on moving destruction followed, never lost
sleep
Ups and downs still a path cleared among thorns
Baptized from birth, a common cause I shared
with a bone
Fully grown, still mingling a concern I noticed
A stranger sees through me, a force behind shines
light
Unknown and unheard there was always a helping
hand
Shaking it off and shunning, in a snap all will be
gone
mother warned

A female bear

Littles ones in tow, A quick glimpse
checking for sneaky foxes
Sharply focused on the thick road ahead
Shrubs and bushes rattle, a warning
to bystanders wanting a quick bite
Heavy breathing and snorting, an alarm
they are aware of
The louder the thuds echos, the clearer
the path in the distance
The young want to play, unaware of
the dangers around
Leaving a trail behind, wolves in
pursuit, incase a cub strays
Through the barren, across open fields, a target
hard to approach

Joe couldn't commit a half grown distracted him
Since then learnt to hunt and hide, search
and sniffle, predators on a prowl
Vulnerable and alone, spend time
grinding my claws
Once in a while I meet a match, my
cuties not for sacriface
Shredding and pummeling, unbeatable in
slitting
Licking my own wounds, the dwarfs love blood
Charging and wrestling an old antelope,
entertainment for the brats
A poked leg slows momentun and invites cowards
Teasing fools, realizes it too late, stuck
between my jaws
The smallest is promising,

worries with gnawning like the father
Watching them grow, a pain knowing any
day an attack is imminent
Going through the usually route,
training their paws and jaws
a sign of encouragement,
battles will be fought and won
As she ages
she takes pride knowing she has nurtured and
molded
a well stabilized legion of conqurers

On your own

A path they followed
A path they travelled
A path they knew well
Two roads at the end of the tunnel,
one is darker and wide
The other narrow and brighter

Unknown to you
Nothing awaits on either side
Only to discover upon arrival
Gutted and fatigued
Behind a hill giggles and laughter
In your face their eyes swell
Sympathetic, false encouragement fills your heart
You wish you had taken the third road
Something they had forgotten to mention
With a clear head, directions given by the
unscrupulous
Lead to nothing but shame
The dilemma that held them back
With hopes of passing onto you
Gives them sleepless nights

You are on your own among the wicked
You are on your own among the selfish
A thirsty man drowns his own and quenches on
soaked garments
A beat up life only has breath to lose
Their gains is in your sufferings
As you surge forward, and as
long as the tree is alive
the leaves will grow

Words from Aunty

Children can be selfish and thoughtless
A neighbour's choice appeals their eyes
Disregarding parents's capabilities
Every mother, father strive to give their
chits the best there is on offer
Pressured guardians self reflect
as the forceful nature matures
creating disturbances
whining and nagging
Turning a peaceful home into
a mud slinging, fiery dumpster
If habits are not curtailed
Rudeness breeds and arrogance
a step away, into oblivion
Given rights are a nourishment for the future
ahead
A task they have already fulfilled
All you want is not what you get
A full stomach is enough love for a brat

Blood is thicker

The building is shaky, marked for destruction
Moulds have deloped
Cracks clearly visible
The steel beams, hell bent with heat
Windows breaking
Water spilling
Soon it will be all over

Heavy machinery closing in
from all directions
Spirited soldiers firing randomly,
instructed to take no prisoners
Erase it to the ground,
from the face of the earth
as if it never existed,
A voice once closer is now distant
Familiar faces stand on side walks
and observe in silence
No emotions, just a deal gone bad,
forgetting the debt they owe
Some are excited,
happy we are on the same page

A dozen employees hold on to cabins,
mortgages on their mind
An earthquake trembles the ruins,
she wants out, when all is good, chickens fly
The lines continue buzzing,
snitches have alerted scroungers

Holding a big file, Mr. Jones budges in,
vowing to take me to the cleaners,

now he is with her
In search of what they don't see,
they have heard of lady Lavoc,
my yatcht in mind

For 30 years carried them on my back
A single misjudge, there is no forgiveness
With grey hair, I look twice my age,
I got to be wise
My one and only mini me,
wishes he could help,
too complicated for his youthful mind
Darkness has activated its tentacles,
I was once untouchable
One look at him, if I slip, he falls,
his fragile bones will break

The ceiling curves in, a last attempt was rejected
On my knees, with a big smile,
I reassure him, papa is no loser
One last call, the call I dreaded,
a lost sibling shows up
The skies open, the sun shines,
a few that stuck by are made partners for life

A leader without a vision, is like an antelope about
to take a drink in a crocodile infested river
Be well and make up, love is us

Blindsided

Glorified by the streets
A persona, of a never drying well
Filled with bubbles of adulations
Splendid in candour,
An admiration of nobles

Kudos to his parents, such nurturing is rare
Fashionable and elegant, his clothes an angels's cut
Blessed with a majestic wit, tall and dignified
Master of his craft
The world in his hand, raptures
and jubilations chase after him

A kindhearted man,
blends well with strangers
Must be favoured in heaven, whispered the less
priviledged
That was his daily mantra,
In public he blossomed
Away from the limelight, alone in his dungeon
A muddled mind, darkened and pear shaped
No space for daylight
Vunerable to his nightmares

In silence, in anguish he crumbled and moaned
Roaches as mates listened in sorrow, feeding on a
frugal meal
Filthy ridden, running out of shows
Passed on a pauper, many came to claim
inheritence
His soul too poor to be shared

Family

Descendants from a common ancestor,
bound by blood and brood
Seeds planted, sprouted, filling out the fields
little ones blindly blinking
Kith and kin
come harvest time, if not properly handled many
will fall off, and some will sprout again, giving
birth to offsprings of the same kind
Given a choice between his murderous heir and a
clean cut stranger, the latter will fall
Never underestimate the power of blood
Blood is not only family, blood is the seed that
stores generational
blood

There can only be one seed for every plant
Hatred and anger is an unfed root
castigating the whole structure
A lost uncle and aunty will return and find
one like them, with their names tatooed on their
chests
What is in the blood cannot be altered
No matter how well you know your
friend, a Maasai is a Maasai
Try as much as you can to preserve the family tree
Mistakes of your ancestors were no mistakes for it
was written
When you find yourselves at crossroads you
might as well practice patience, your unborn will
resemble them

Bug

Every woman has dreams of a big family
Every man has dreams of a happy life

During the course of time, formalities
and principles are adhered to
If you fall under that category,
you are well cultivated enough to live a perfect life
You would have excelled, surpassed and
flourished in various disciplines
Your hopes and head are held high up
With your feet firmly on the ground,
ready for the next take off
Mama's girl is not only intelligent,
she is cultural and traditional, a gift for a seeker

With a perfectly built platform only a
suitable match ready to shoot for
the moon is scouted for
Nurtured and matured, prepared
to fill a playground

Nuptials tied befitting a royal gathering
Six months down the line a bug creeps
out shattering what would have been a
dedicated marriage, so is with the
ways of this world
There is never a guarante only hope and
faith shall carry us through
Never be afraid to try again
Never give up For the devil knows
our intials but not our names

Man up

I wondered if I was adopted or taken in,
I had to be rock solid, impenetrable
I took it with my chin up
Got so used to it, I craved for more
Sleeping was about thinking of the next task
Chilling was castrating bulls and hunting wild pigs
My feet have seen places I dare not talk about
Covered in scratches and blisters a
sign I can get down
Out of the blue the torments and abuse
ceased, to my regret I had become accustomed to it

I was elevated to a man, equiped with every
son's dream, a proud father
Given responsibilities and put in charge of men
I stood shook and confused, how could
I jump from a slave to a leader
Not knowing it was part of a bigger plan
With a nod and a pat, I was warned again
If anything goes wrong, you are in deep trouble
There was no trouble bigger than what
I had experienced
I grinned hoping trouble would come
soon for I had learnt from a master who
had mastered my father
One rule tears can only be of joy

Thoughts

Among the many bushes, not all thongs are thongs , if
you look carefully some plants have taken the form of
their host
So is with humanity, you cannot be humble living
with scavengers, for they will mistake you for a dead
body

Be watchfull when others talk, when you feel
burdened walk away silently, fists fly easily

Being alone does not necessary mean you are lost, a
crowd tend to want the best of you

No one can pretend to know you, everyone have their
own idol

Influence discovered in infancy, makes you shine for
a while

Think deep and be youself, there is always a ticking
in you

Some are shaped by thier upbringing, becareful when
you approach them, their best is usually reserved for
fools

What could have been great minds fall short among
the brave and the dedicated

Rushing to get there is like a disease that cannot be
contained, when the vaccine comes it gets flushed out
like a flea caught in the wind

Soaring to great heights without a taint of a scar leaves you
with a childish nostalgia

If you are lucky enough to be an elite, at a younger age
remember great accomplishments are achieved through
resilience

Regrets of the past are a mirror for future problems, don't
look back someone is watching you and they can see where
you are going

As hard as it is to believe, to love and be loved is a question
disputed by the heart and discussed by the brain, very often

She reflected and speculated about all the different versions associated with the German culture. She concluded that several members of the minority groups had misguided personal issues regarding ways and mentality of certain German individuals and organizations. A lot might have lacked the skills and education to find a decent job or did not possess the necessary permits required. And that led to biased assumptions and disdain for the hosting nation. The inflexibility and the intolerance or slow to adjust coupled with a never bending bureaucratic system led to a habit of blame game while questioning their unfair treatment. Most of the victims had inherited negative tendencies and attitudes passed on, from their guardians, associates and cultural institutes. Germans are no different from any other nationalities, it's just that they don't know it any other way. Their beliefs, their patriotism and principals are based on the expression, a leopard cannot change its spots. They are deeply embedded and permanent, unless certain adjustments or miracle spiritual cleansing are carried out before birth.

However, being adventurers and venturing into unfamiliar territories leads to experimental tests and weakened dilution. You could sprinkle ashes all over or spray paint on some parts, but when cornered, they can easily shake off these ashes and reveal themselves, or with time the paint will fade away and if not constantly recoated, it can unmask its true colors. But one thing for sure is that they remain resolute, mentally strong, focused, and unbearable.

Typical "Die Mannschaft mentality," as Dr. Matthias once said profoundly. This resentment came by not because of the hurt, but because of the history, that was created long before they were born. The sins of their great grandmothers who bore the unwanted kids that overwhelmed and asphyxiated the rest of the tadpoles, and be born a nightmare.

A lot managed to escape and overpower the zealots, but were born marked with regret, as they never wanted to be part of it. Up to now they despise themselves and those that are like them, but they can never be anything else.

They find solace in being as far away as possible, eliminating any signs of remembrance and preventing any flashbacks.

Alcohol is addictive and it makes life easier. Certain parts dissect from your body and become what you have always wanted to be, while the other parts fall in anger into soft folds, as they observe in disgust their stubborn self migrate into forbidden lands. They wait impatiently and awkwardly for the loose souls to return and become whole again. By now, they are used to it, for they are aware its only for short periods, that is if they don't mingle with the Bavarian brothers.

Her thoughts were destructed by a familiar voice. When she turned around, she saw Kyra with dyed black hair rushing out of the hotel surrounded by three men. She assumed they were guests at the same hotel, but the receptionist told her the name didn't exist in their computers.

When she got to her room, the whole place had been ransacked, her clothes thrown all over.
She was in panic and could not report the incident, afraid the police would be called in.

She had placed a small bag with her fortune in a hot water dispenser and it was still intact, she sighed with relief and sat down trying to calm her nerves.

After a while she got up, left the hotel and disappeared in the middle of midnight.

Quotes

"*Don't fall in love, be loved.*"

"*In the dark every shadow is mysterious.*"

"*If all I had was you in this world, it would be enough.*"

Something strange out there

At the edge of a long dark road, a mysterious
breeze whispered silently. My gaze was darkened
by the charcoal fumes swirling nearby. It was al-
most midnight not a single soul in sight. A journey I
was trully terrified to take.
The longer I remained idle, the darker and scary
it became, "I should have stayed on that bus," I
murmed softly.
My mind was racing, I could feel the cold sweat on
my back. A voice urged me, "you have to get home,
mama would be angry."
With my eyes closed and my heart in my hands I
pushed myself forward. Not realizing I was shaking
with fear. The crunchy gravel road gave me away.
I stayed still listening if I had attracted attention.
My pounding heart was louder than a beat box.
I tried to conceal it, but it was to no avail. Suddenly
I began to run, I could not see a metre in front of
me. I tripped over a rock and fell, bruising my el-
bows and knees. As I got up, I caught sight of some-
one walking in front of me. With delight, I quickly
brushed myself and followed him but I didn't want
to be too close.

I walked slowly and in silence. I noticed that the
slower I got, the more closer he came to me.
Soon I found myself walking side by side with him.
"What are you doing here this time of the night?"
My hair stood, goose bumps enveloped my body.
It was a voice not from this planet, but I was too
young and innocent to know. I thought it was bea-
cause I was scared and in a hurry to get home.

"I am coming from playing basket ball and I missed my bus, that's why I am so late. Don't you know that it's dangerous to move around during this time of the night. What is basket ball anyway.

Uh it's a game where you play with a round ball, passing to each other and shooting in the basket.

You mean like netball, I used to play that game during my time. I was confused what he meant by during his time, but then I again I thought better of it. Ususally netball was played by women, that's when I realized I could not tell whether it was a woman or a man. As we walked, the wind and the leaves rustled behind us. It sounded like an army of warriors following behind. Although it was dark, shadows emerged and disappeared into darkerness.
" Which family do you belong too." I told him my father's name and he said, " that is the reason I was sent here."
I thought maybe my mother is the one who had sent him, since my dad had died ten years ago.
He repeated again the same questions more than five times.
"Why are you walking during the time of the hour? Don't you know that it is dangerous?"
I answered with the same answers until we where a short distance from begining of the streets lights. He warned me not to ever walk alone during the night and told me to run home and not to look back. I ran a few steps and looked back, to my surprise he just melted into the dark. I did not stop until

nor look back again until I got home. As soon as I opened the door, I asked my mum why she had sent such a weird person to escort me.

She stopped what she was doing and stared at me.

" Eat your food before it gets cold and go to sleep."

I did as I was told. After three days my mum asked me to explain again what had happened that same day. I narrated the whole story and she said to me.

"I don't want you to be scared. I did not sent anyone to fetch you and the person you just described, he was not from this world.

Quotes

"*Inspiration creates possibilities if movement is encouraged.*"

"*Guidance without commitment and expecting a favourable result violets the verdict.*"

"*Pyschology is the master of all evils.*"

www.ingramcontent.com/pod-product-compliance
Lightning Source LLC
LaVergne TN
LVHW011034200726
843509LV00011B/1275